PBR

A Pillar Box Red Publication

in association with

MATCH! & **World Soccer**

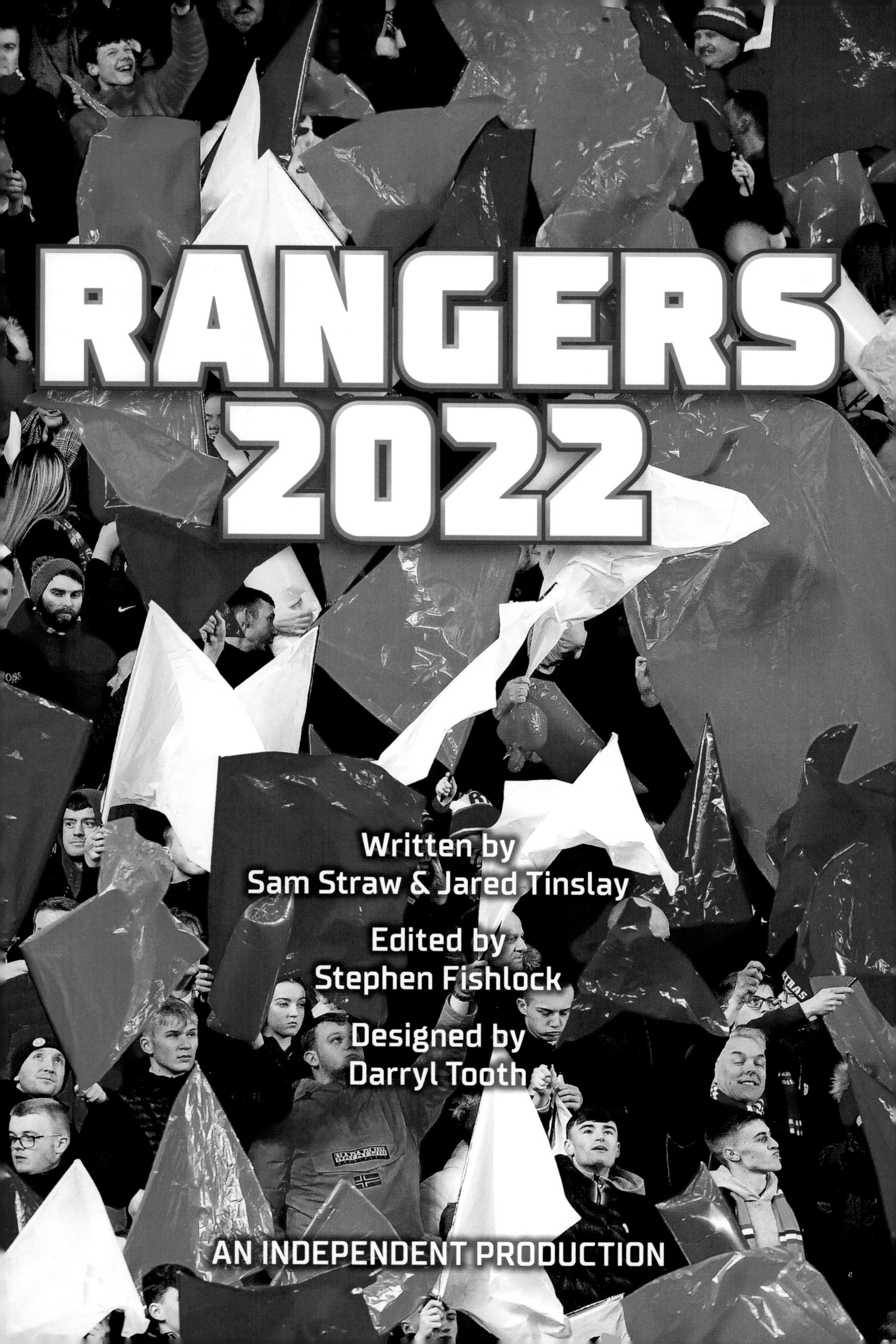

RANGERS 2022

Written by
Sam Straw & Jared Tinslay

Edited by
Stephen Fishlock

Designed by
Darryl Tooth

AN INDEPENDENT PRODUCTION

CONTENTS

8 Season Review 2020–21

14 The Invincibles

16 He Said What?

17 Ryan Kent Poster

18 Quiz 1

20 Ibrox In Numbers

22 Steven Gerrard's Rangers Scrapbook

26 Quiz 2

28 Gers Stars Revealed

30 Competition

32 Follow MATCH

33 John Lundstram Poster

34 YouTube Clips

36 Quiz 3

38 Old Firm History

40 Rangers Legends

42 Rangers Board Game: Become A Legend

43 Steven Davis Poster

44 Quiz 4

46 Stat Attack

48 Rangers' Next Generation

50 Subscribe To World Soccer

51 Joe Aribo Poster

52 Quiz 5

54 2021–22 First Team Squad

55 2021–22 Home Kit

56 Design Your Gers Kit

58 Subscribe To MATCH

59 Connor Goldson Poster

60 Quiz Answers

62 Roll Of Honour

SEASON REVIEW

We look back at Rangers' 2020–21 title-winning campaign month by month, checking out their biggest moments, star players and more!

AUGUST

MEGA MOMENTS!

Roofe joins The Gers

On the same day that Rangers' 2019–20 Europa League journey came to an end against Bayer Leverkusen in Germany, The Gers completed the signings of former Leeds striker Kemar Roofe from Anderlecht and Swiss ace Cedric Itten from St. Gallen. They both added significant firepower to Steven Gerrard's squad at Ibrox!

Morelos stays at Ibrox

Roofe and Itten may have signed, but there was intense speculation that fellow striker Alfredo Morelos would be leaving Ibrox! Despite being heavily linked with the likes of Porto and Lille, the Colombian hitman ended up staying in Scotland. He didn't let the rumours distract him either, as he smashed home five goals in the first seven games of the season. Mega deadly!

Despite the disappointment of being knocked out of the 2019–20 Europa League by Bayer Leverkusen 4–1 on aggregate, The Gers made an unbeaten start to the 2020–21 Scottish Prem, winning five of their six games in August. Not only that, but they were scoring plenty of goals in the process, beating both St. Mirren and St. Johnstone 3–0!

Kent celebrates with his team-mates

MAN OF THE MONTH!

RYAN KENT The ex-Liverpool winger has turned out to be one of Steven Gerrard's best signings at Ibrox. He started off the season in inspirational form as he picked up three goals and two assists in the first six league games of the campaign!

DID YOU KNOW?

Rangers' six clean sheets in their opening six games equalled the record set by Celtic 115 years ago. Wow!

RANGERS' RESULTS

Date	Comp	Home	Score	Away
01/08	SP	Aberdeen	0–1	Rangers
06/08	EL	Bayer Leverkusen	1–0	Rangers
09/08	SP	Rangers	3–0	St. Mirren
12/08	SP	Rangers	3–0	St. Johnstone
16/08	SP	Livingston	0–0	Rangers
22/08	SP	Rangers	2–0	Kilmarnock
29/08	SP	Hamilton Acad.	0–2	Rangers

SEPTEMBER
MEGA MOMENTS!

Off to a Flyer in Europe

Steven Gerrard was keen for his side to go further in the 2020–21 Europa League, and his players made a good start with convincing wins against Lincoln Red Imps and Willem II in qualifying. Those two wins left them with just Galatasaray to beat in order to reach the group stage!

Four-goal thriller

After notching up their seventh clean sheet in their first seven league games with a 4–0 win against Dundee United at Ibrox, Hibernian were the first team to score against Rangers in the Scottish Prem in a four-goal thriller in the following game!

Comfortable

Gerrard's Gers bounced back from dropping points against Hibernian by beating Motherwell 5–1 at Fir Park! James Tavernier and Cedric Itten both scored braces, while Jordan Jones scored his first goal for the club in a comfortable victory!

MAN OF THE MONTH!

JAMES TAVERNIER As well as scoring a double from the spot against Motherwell, the rampaging right-back also netted against Dundee United and in the Europa League qualifiers against Lincoln Red Imps and Willem II! The full-back's trademark deliveries were also proving to be a key attacking weapon for Steven Gerrard's men going forward!

DID YOU KNOW?

Nobody on the pitch had more touches than James Tavernier in Rangers' 5–1 win against Motherwell!

RANGERS' RESULTS

Date	Comp	Home	Score	Away
12/09	SP	Rangers	4-0	Dundee United
17/09	EL	Lincoln Red Imps	0-5	Rangers
20/09	SP	Hibernian	2-2	Rangers
24/09	EL	Willem II	0-4	Rangers
27/09	SP	Motherwell	1-5	Rangers

OCTOBER
MEGA MOMENTS!

Rangers beat Galatasaray

After comfortable wins against Lincoln Red Imps and Willem II, Rangers knew they just needed to beat Galatasaray to qualify for the group stage of the Europa League – and they did just that! Goals by Scott Arfield and James Tavernier were enough to see The Gers reach the group stage of the competition for a third consecutive season!

RANGERS' RESULTS

Date	Comp	Home	Score	Away
01/10	EL	Rangers	2-1	Galatasaray
04/10	SP	Rangers	2-0	Ross County
17/10	SP	Celtic	0-2	Rangers
22/10	EL	Standard Liege	0-2	Rangers
25/10	SP	Rangers	2-0	Livingston
29/10	EL	Rangers	1-0	Lech Poznan

Old Firm

The Gers continued their sensational start to the Scottish Premiership season by picking up another three victories without conceding a single goal, including a 2–0 win against bitter rivals Celtic in the first Old Firm derby of the season!

Wondergoal

Not only were Rangers flying in the Scottish Prem, but they were totally rocking the Europa League too! The Gers picked up class wins v Standard Liege and Lech Poznan in Group D. If you haven't already, make sure you check out Kemar Roofe's outrageous halfway-line goal against Standard Liege!

MAN OF THE MONTH!

CONNOR GOLDSON Even though there were tons of contenders for Rangers' Player of the Month for October, we simply had to pick defender Goldson! As well as helping his side keep another five clean sheets, he scored both goals against Celtic to cement himself into Rangers folklore. Legend!

DID YOU KNOW?

Celtic didn't even manage a shot on target against Rangers in the first Old Firm derby of the season!

NOVEMBER

MEGA MOMENTS!

Thriller

After starting the month with a 1-0 win against Kilmarnock in the Scottish Prem, Rangers were involved in a six-goal thriller with Benfica in the Europa League! The Gers were denied a famous win in Portugal by two late goals from the hosts!

Things continued to get better and better for Rangers in the Scottish Prem as they battered Hamilton Academical 8-0 at Ibrox and stuffed Aberdeen 4-0 to end the month with a mega healthy lead over Celtic in the race for the title!

Rangers beat Hamilton 8-0

Arfield bags v Benfica

Goals continued to flow for The Gers as they ended the month with another thriller against Benfica at Ibrox, before beating Falkirk 4-0 in the second round of the Scottish League Cup! They were on flames!

RANGERS' RESULTS

01/11	SP	Kilmarnock	0-1	Rangers
05/11	EL	Benfica	3-3	Rangers
08/11	SP	Rangers	8-0	Hamilton Acad.
22/11	SP	Rangers	4-0	Aberdeen
26/11	EL	Rangers	2-2	Benfica
29/11	SLC	Falkirk	0-4	Rangers

MAN OF THE MONTH!

JAMES TAVERNIER Similarly to October's gong, we struggled to single out one player for Rangers' Player of the Month for November. However, Tavernier's impressive return of both goals and assists meant we had to give him the award again!

DID YOU KNOW?

Rangers' 8-0 win against Hamilton Academical was their biggest victory under manager Steven Gerrard!

DECEMBER

MEGA MOMENTS!

If Rangers were expecting a bit of a breather from a relentless schedule over Christmas, they couldn't have been more wrong! The Gers had nine games to get through in the month of December, but still managed to win all six of their league games to extend their lead at the top of the Scottish Prem. Total heroes!

Table-toppers

It wasn't all plain sailing for The Gers in December, though – St. Mirren scored a dramatic injury-time winner to end Rangers' 27-game unbeaten start to the season and knock them out of the Scottish League Cup in the process!

Upset

MAN OF THE MONTH!

KEMAR ROOFE Although James Tavernier had another good month, Kemar Roofe's five league goals were crucial in helping The Gers enjoy another perfect month in the Scottish Prem!

DID YOU KNOW?

Kemar Roofe's five goals in the Scottish Premiership in December came from a total of 17 shots!

Wins against Standard Liege and Lech Poznan saw Rangers finish top of Group D in the Europa League! Goals from Cedric Itten and Ianis Hagi in their final group game ensured that they finished two points above Benfica!

European progress

RANGERS' RESULTS

03/12	EL	Rangers	3-2	Standard Liege
06/12	SP	Ross County	0-4	Rangers
10/12	EL	Lech Poznan	0-2	Rangers
13/12	SP	Dundee United	1-2	Rangers
16/12	SLC	St. Mirren	3-2	Rangers
19/12	SP	Rangers	3-1	Motherwell
23/12	SP	St. Johnstone	0-3	Rangers
26/12	SP	Rangers	1-0	Hibernian
30/12	SP	St. Mirren	0-2	Rangers

JANUARY
MEGA MOMENTS!

Old Firm

Morelos celebrates

What better way of celebrating the New Year than getting one over your bitter rivals? That's exactly what Rangers did as they exploited Celtic's vulnerable defence in a dramatic Old Firm derby at Ibrox. An own-goal from Callum McGregor was all there was to separate the two teams!

Rangers didn't have any Europa League games to contend with in January, so they could fully focus on their title charge! They moved 22 points clear at the top of the table after beating Aberdeen 2-1 at Pittodrie, before being held to a draw away at Motherwell!

Party time

Steven Gerrard's men ended the month with two more important wins against Ross County and Hibernian. The 5-0 win against Ross County was particularly impressive, with five different goalscorers getting themselves on the scoresheet. Lethal!

RANGERS' RESULTS

02/01	SP	Rangers	1-0	Celtic
10/01	SP	Aberdeen	1-2	Rangers
17/01	SP	Motherwell	1-1	Rangers
23/01	SP	Rangers	5-0	Ross County
27/01	SP	Hibernian	0-1	Rangers

MAN OF THE MONTH!

JOE ARIBO Not only did he score one and assist another in January, but Joe Aribo was a key player in another near perfect month for Rangers in the Scottish Premiership. He also completed eight successful dribbles which helped him make the Scottish Prem Team of the Month!

DID YOU KNOW?

Alfredo Morelos scored two vital goals against Aberdeen and another against Hibernian in January, taking his goal tally for 2020-21 into double figures!

FEBRUARY
MEGA MOMENTS!

Hagi scores v St. Johnstone

Rangers began February with two 1-0 victories against St. Johnstone and Kilmarnock in the Scottish Prem either side of a frustrating draw with Hamilton. If it wasn't for a 94th-minute equaliser from Hamilton, then Rangers would have enjoyed another perfect month under Steven Gerrard!

The highlight of February, however, for Rangers was undoubtedly the two wins against Royal Antwerp in the Europa League! The Gers won 4-3 away in Belgium before winning the return leg at Ibrox 5-2! It secured a 9-5 aggregate win and their place in the round of 16 for a second consecutive season!

Rangers beat Royal Antwerp

In between the two dramatic games at Royal Antwerp, Rangers picked up another valuable three points in the Scottish Prem with a 4-1 victory against Dundee United at Ibrox to move within seven points of winning the league!

Dundee United sunk

MAN OF THE MONTH!

ALFREDO MORELOS With two jaw-dropping Man of the Match displays for Rangers against Royal Antwerp in the Europa League, we couldn't look past Morelos! The Colombian was a constant menace and was key to his side's progression!

DID YOU KNOW?

Over the two legs against Royal Antwerp, Alfredo Morelos was involved in eight of Rangers' nine goals!

RANGERS' RESULTS

03/02	SP	Rangers	1-0	St. Johnstone
07/02	SP	Hamilton Acad.	1-1	Rangers
13/02	SP	Rangers	1-0	Kilmarnock
18/02	EL	Royal Antwerp	3-4	Rangers
21/02	SP	Rangers	4-1	Dundee United
25/02	EL	Rangers	5-2	Royal Antwerp

MARCH

MEGA MOMENTS!

Celebrations in George Square

After starting March with two wins in the Scottish Prem against Livingston and St. Mirren, Rangers officially won their 55th Scottish top-flight title after Celtic's goalless draw with Dundee United! Not only did they reclaim the title, but they denied Celtic the opportunity to make it ten-in-a-row!

RANGERS' RESULTS

03/03	SP	Livingston	0-1	Rangers
06/03	SP	Rangers	3-0	St. Mirren
11/03	EL	Slavia Prague	1-1	Rangers
18/03	EL	Rangers	0-2	Slavia Prague
21/03	SP	Celtic	1-1	Rangers

Slavia Prague too strong

It was too much to ask for Rangers to progress to the quarter-finals of the Europa League in the same month, though, with Slavia Prague beating The Gers 2-0 in the second leg at Ibrox to end the Scottish side's Europa League dreams for 2020-21!

Morelos nets v Celtic

However, The Gers remained on course for an unbeaten season in the Scottish Prem as they drew 1-1 with Celtic to end the month on a high. That being said, their failure to win denied them the chance to beat Celtic's 106-point haul in their 2016-17 campaign!

MAN OF THE MONTH!

ALFREDO MORELOS Given that Morelos netted in all three league matches that The Gers played in March, we couldn't not give this award to the Colombian! On top of his goals, he also made a massive contribution with his general play!

DID YOU KNOW?

Alfredo Morelos' first-half strike for Rangers against Celtic was his first goal in 13 Old Firm derbies. Mad!

APRIL

MEGA MOMENTS!

Roofe scores against Cove Rangers

Kemar Roofe's brace helped Rangers begin April with a 4-0 win against Cove Rangers in the Scottish Cup and set up another meeting with arch-rivals Celtic in the next round! They also kept their hopes of remaining unbeaten in the league for the entire season alive with a 2-1 win against Hibernian!

RANGERS' RESULTS

04/04	SC	Rangers	4-0	Cove Rangers
11/04	SP	Rangers	2-1	Hibernian
18/04	SC	Rangers	2-0	Celtic
21/04	SP	St. Johnstone	1-1	Rangers
25/04	SC	Rangers	1-1	St. Johnstone*

*St. Johnstone win 4-2 on penalties

Rangers beat Celtic

The Gers heaped more misery onto Celtic by beating them 2-0 at Ibrox in the fourth round of the Scottish Cup. Steven Davis' overhead kick and a Jonjoe Kenny own goal was enough to see Gerrard's side progress to the next round!

St. Johnstone

After being held to a 1-1 draw by St. Johnstone in the Scottish Prem, Rangers ended the month by being knocked out of the Scottish Cup themselves by the same opposition a few days later on penalties! Rangers looked to have won the game in extra-time when James Tavernier struck in the 117th minute, but Chris Kane equalised for the visitors just minutes later!

MAN OF THE MONTH!

KEMAR ROOFE Although there were no standout contenders for Player of the Month in April, Kemar Roofe's two classy goals against Cove Rangers and an assist against Hibernian make him a worthy winner. What a signing he turned out to be!

DID YOU KNOW?

Rangers' 2-0 Scottish Cup win v Celtic condemned their rivals to their first trophyless season since 2010!

SCOTTISH PREMIERSHIP CHAMPIONS 2020/21

Rangers lift the trophy

MAY

MEGA MOMENTS!

Roofe celebrates v Celtic

Rangers showed why they deserved to win the title with a third Old Firm derby league win of the season in their opening game in May! Kemar Roofe's double along with goals from Alfredo Morelos and Jermain Defoe heaped further misery onto ten-man Celtic!

The Gers followed that up with another comfortable victory away at Livingston, courtesy of goals from James Tavernier, Ryan Kent and Ianis Hagi! That left The Gers with just one game to remain unbeaten for the entire season in the Scottish Prem. Wow!

Rangers fans party

Unsurprisingly, Steven Gerrard's players completed their 'Invincible' season with a 4–0 win against Aberdeen at Ibrox on the final day! The Gers became the first team to go unbeaten since Brendan Rodgers' Celtic in 2016–17, and also matched Celtic's 107-year-old clean sheet record. Heroes!

Celebrating v Aberdeen

MAN OF THE MONTH!

KEMAR ROOFE After netting a brace against arch-rivals Celtic, striker Kemar Roofe picked up another double on the final day against Aberdeen! He remained clinical throughout the entire season for The Gers and was a key reason behind why they were able to end Celtic's dominance in Scotland!

DID YOU KNOW?

The 13 goals Rangers conceded in the 2020–21 Scottish Premiership set a new league record, beating Celtic's previous record of 14 in 1913–14!

RANGERS' RESULTS

Date	Comp	Home	Score	Away
02/05	SP	Rangers	4-1	Celtic
12/05	SP	Livingston	0-3	Rangers
15/05	SP	Rangers	4-0	Aberdeen

1903

They secured the title as early as March 7 – that's the earliest a Scottish title has been won since 1903!

THE INVIN

Rangers went the entire league season unbeaten as they lifted their 55th Scottish Premiership trophy in 2020-21, so we've picked out some of the best stats and facts behind their title-winning campaign...

26 They kept a whopping 26 clean sheets as they beat the Scottish clean-sheet record for a 38-game season set by Celtic in 2014-15!

11 Ianis Hagi got 11 assists in the 2020-21 Scottish Prem - more than any player in the league!

14 Striker Kemar Roofe finished as Rangers' top goalscorer in the league with 14 strikes!

25 They ended the season 25 points clear of bitter rivals Celtic. Wowzers!

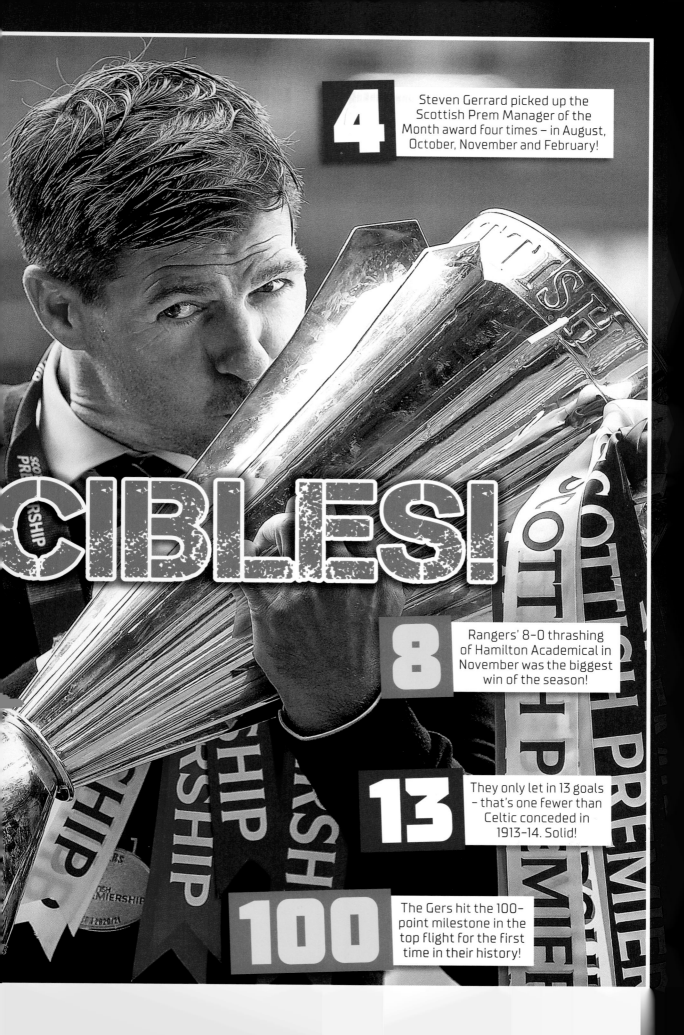

CIBLES!

4 Steven Gerrard picked up the Scottish Prem Manager of the Month award four times – in August, October, November and February!

8 Rangers' 8–0 thrashing of Hamilton Academical in November was the biggest win of the season!

13 They only let in 13 goals – that's one fewer than Celtic conceded in 1913–14. Solid!

100 The Gers hit the 100-point milestone in the top flight for the first time in their history!

"This is a special team. You won't come across many teams like this in football where everybody wants the best for everybody. We put it to bed early, but we didn't stop there. We went unbeaten and put ourselves in the history books!"

Ryan Kent has become a key player at Ibrox since joining from Liverpool in 2018!

"When I first came in I wanted to put the club where it belonged. It's taken longer than I expected but I couldn't ask for a better season from the boys with what they've done. Everything added on to that, we've brought pride back home to the club and it's such an amazing feeling!"

Skipper James Tavernier proved all of the doubters wrong with a sensational season at Ibrox!

HE SAID WHAT?

"I have dedicated my whole career and my whole life for these kinds of moments. I always knew it would happen at some point in my career and that is the thing that has kept me going to be honest."

It's fair to say that Jermain Defoe was buzzing to win his first-ever league title!

Get a load of some of our fave Rangers quotes after the title was secured!

"Was this part of the vision the gaffer sold to me when I signed back in 2018? Yeah, it was. Did I think it would be three years later? Probably not."

Connor Goldson didn't expect gaffer Steven Gerrard to deliver on his vision so early at Rangers!

"It still feels really good, the game takes you to some incredible highs but it also takes you to some real lows as well and we've had to come through that. But to do it in the style we did it, to dominate the league the way the players did it, I think it's going to feel good for a long time!"

Gaffer Steven Gerrard will want his players to remember the feeling of lifting the trophy to keep them motivated!

"I learned right away how important this season was for the club. Every day somebody was telling me about 55, and it got to the point where it stuck and I was telling people about 55!"

Kemar Roofe's goals made him an instant hit at Rangers!

KENT

FACTPACK

Name: Ryan Kent

D.O.B: 11 November, 1996

Position: Winger

Country: England

Strongest Foot: Right

Top Skill: Rapid dribbling!

Boot Brand: Nike

WORDSEARCH

Can you find all 27 of Rangers' 2020-21 squad members in this grid?

```
P L B W Z B N G R N C X U Y A E G G M C T H X H R J I R K D
F J Q B J F Z J F X Y P J H E L A N D E R B Z A P C L C L L
H J G G I O J C P M C Z M P W Q I G J M C F A U Z Y Q X P E
Y U T P L R G Z Q K U H V X Y L F L L T D A N S F Z W Q F I
W M C I J U L V U A H N K C H K I N H L J J C L S C V O X W
W C V P G A E E W D I W G G P B C L U C F Z P C V E O G Q G
Q P Z G U P B G A G E T U S T Y D B K C C K I N G R Y W I O
Q L W Q F J D G E U O A T Z L W P G M C G R E G O R B Q Z O
C F T U P R C P A S L K F E R C X U I H U Z H Z W S Y E J A
P R X P Q V T J X C X D T V N V D W D P V C J A C K Q E K Y
C G W Y H A Y X M A E T P Y U G P C N R Z J K A M A R A U D
K N J V Y W R C C W G N A P T N L K D T F M R A P L W G Z E
L I G L V O Q I M L O S W V S H N Q U C C F P X E K B E U F
P Y R P I V E V B K L B Y Y E Y O V L G O Y K G E J V C N O
P Q S O R Z Y T L O D P U P R R D B N O N C C M R G T F G E
W M I O S S J X J H S C C K C W N F A G S N E Q X S B I U T
W T R D O R I Y K J O T D U E C G I W R P A P D I U N R L E
Y W H H X S L M B Y N B B G H N C T E X V L L J A E B T O P
N R R D A B F F P V J Z B M V G T O O R Y F K B V H L H X H
Q O Q I Y G E N A S P C U W S F C Q Y V K Q L J O R B Q X N
J P X E G E I Y R X O W Y D G K Q R S H U L S T E W A R T G
G G P P H H W R F G S N X M O V W P S M H T M D M S L A F W
G R V L Z W T E I M J P W V S K O O V E C Z B A E C O S G Y
M Y C K K E K S E K A J J Q S W L S M J S X R V C P G F B W
S Q W T B P A E L E Z K C I P E B J V S W Z U I Z M U E Q M
B J E V T T U D P A T T E R S O N Z P P V S S D F N Q R A
P E J U E Y I M N A N C G O R I M P M Q N I J H T G O G V N
H K Z D W Z C U H C V J M H E G A N Q Y R Y X I M R U T P U
S J R S J E P O X V M W A E B I G P L A Y E L M B H Z I F X
J A B Y F C P B G H Y G O C R K V R B Y G D N X T G O H W T
```

Arfield	Defoe	Jack	McLaughlin	Tavernier
Aribo	Firth	Kamara	Morelos	Wright
Balogun	Goldson	Katic	Patterson	Zungu
Barisic	Hagi	Kent	Roofe	
Bassey	Helander	King	Simpson	
Davis	Itten	McGregor	Stewart	

ACTION REPLAY

How much can you remember about Rangers' 4-1 hammering of arch-rivals Celtic last season?

1 What competition did this Old Firm clash take place in – the Scottish Prem or cup?

2 Who played in goal for Rangers – Allan McGregor or Jon McLaughlin?

3 True or False? Odsonne Edouard missed the match through injury!

4 Name the class Rangers striker who opened the scoring in the 26th minute!

5 What was the score at half-time at Ibrox?

6 How did Jermain Defoe score in stoppage time – a penalty, free-kick or from open play?

7 Who got sent off for Celtic in the first half – Scott Brown, Greg Taylor or Callum McGregor?

8 True or False? Celtic scored with their only shot on target!

9 Which team had more possession of the ball – Rangers or Celtic?

ANSWERS ON PAGE 60

IBROX IN NUMBERS

Check out all the stats behind Rangers' jaw-dropping stadium!

1899
The year the mega stadium officially opened!

'18
The number of times Ibrox has been a home venue for the Scotland national team – the third most of any ground!

2014
It was used for the 2014 Commonwealth Games in Glasgow!

50,817
The current capacity of Ibrox!

57,000

Plans to increase the stadium's capacity to 57,000 were prevented from going ahead due to the financial crisis and the club's administration!

118,567

The record attendance at Ibrox for an Old Firm derby in 1939!

3

It's the third biggest stadium in Scotland!

105M X 68M

The size of the pitch at Ibrox!

STEVEN GERARD'S...
RANGERS

JOINING THE GERS
May 2018
The former Liverpool midfielder replaced interim manager Graeme Murty as Rangers gaffer to begin his spell at the club! Since retiring as a player, he'd been working as a youth coach at Anfield, but said he was "honoured" to take over The Gers!

DREAM DEBUT
July 2018
Stevie G kicked off his Rangers reign with a hard-fought 2-0 victory over Macedonians Shkupi in Europa League qualifying! Jamie Murphy's low first-half finish was the first-ever goal scored under their new boss!

FIRST UNBEATEN RUN
September 2018
Under Gerrard's guidance, The Gers went 12 matches unbeaten in all competitions from the start of the 2018-19 season, but eventually suffered defeat against their old enemies Celtic in the first Old Firm clash of the season!

BHOYS BEATEN
December 2018
In the reverse fixture with Celtic later that year, Gerrard's side got sweet revenge with a 1-0 victory over their arch rivals! It was Rangers' first win over their city neighbours since 2012 – a rut that had stretched for over six years!

Scrapbook!

We track Steven Gerrard's journey so far as Rangers manager – since taking charge of the club in 2018 to the present day!

MANAGER OF THE MONTH

April 2019

After getting four wins from four in April 2019, the ex-England captain won his first-ever Manager of the Month award and became the first Rangers boss to win the prize since they returned to the Premiership in 2016! He went on to win another six ahead of the 2021–22 season!

LOYAL LEADER

July 2019

After leading The Gers to their highest points total since returning to the Premiership in 2016, loads of reports suggested Gerrard was Newcastle's first choice to take over from Rafa Benitez! According to spies, Gerrard turned down a move to the Prem because he was happy at Rangers!

December 2019

By finishing second behind Portuguese giants Porto in the Europa League's Group G during the 2019-20 campaign, Gerrard became the first Rangers manager to successfully navigate the club through the group stage of a major European competition since Paul Le Guen way back in 2006-07. Legend!

EUROPA LEAGUE

NEW DEAL

December 2019

The big bosses at Ibrox were clearly over the moon with Gerrard's progress, so they handed him a two-year contract extension that extended his stay at the club until 2024. What a wicked early Christmas present!

EPIC AWAY DAY

December 2019

At the end of December, a second-half goal from centre-back Nikola Katic sealed Rangers their first away victory over Celtic in the Scottish Premiership for nine years. Wowzers!

RECORD WIN

November 2020

Ruthless Rangers recorded their biggest-ever win under Gerrard – an 8-0 victory v Hamilton Academical! It was the biggest victory since the Scottish Premiership was re-branded in 2013 and the largest margin of victory in the league that season!

THE INVINCIBLES

May 2021

Rangers eased to a 4-0 win over Aberdeen on the final gameweek to end the season unbeaten! They became just the fourth team in world footy to go a 38+ game top-flight campaign unbeaten this century, and also smashed the 100-point barrier for the first time in a 38-game season!

THE CHAMPIONS

March 2021

The Gers won their 55th Scottish top-flight title after Celtic failed to beat Dundee! It ended their rivals' hopes of winning ten league titles in a row, and saw Gerrard seal his first piece of silverware since taking over as manager!

MANAGER OF THE YEAR

May 2021

Gerrard deservedly completed a personal treble after being named PFA Scotland Manager of the Year, SPFL Manager of the Year and collecting the Scottish Football Writers' Association prize as well. Hero!

SPOT THE DIFFERENCE

Study these Rangers v Aberdeen pictures really carefully, then see if you can find the ten differences between them!

NAME THE TEAM

Can you remember the stars that lined up in Rangers' 5-2 win against Royal Antwerp in last season's Europa League?

1. Left-back

2. Midfielder

3. Right-back

4. Centre-back

5. Centre-back

6. Goalkeeper

7. Winger

8. Striker

9. Midfielder

10. Midfielder

11. Winger

ANSWERS ON PAGE 60

GERS ST

We've got some epic inside information you might not already know about your favourite Rangers heroes!

ROOFE

As well as bagging tons of goals, the epic striker also loves gaming in his spare time. Just look at that set-up!

GERRARD

When he was dominating in midfield for Liverpool during his playing days, Rangers boss Stevie G was described as one of the greatest by Ronaldinho. Hero!

TAVERNIER

The right-back was born in Bradford, West Yorkshire, and joined Leeds United's youth system when he was just nine!

SAKALA

By joining Rangers, Fashion Sakala has become the first-ever Zambian star to play in the Scottish Prem. Hero!

McGREGOR

Nobody has made more appearances for The Gers in Europe than epic GK Allan McGregor!

LUNDSTRAM

John's sister Jodie is seven years older than him and a well-known actress. Cool!

ARS revealed!

HAGI

Ianis' dad is legendary footballer Gheorghe Hagi – he played for both Real Madrid and Barcelona. Baller!

MORELOS

Rangers signed Alfredo Morelos for just £1 million from HJK in 2017. Bargain!

ARFIELD

Arfield switched his international allegiance from Scotland to Canada in March 2016 and became captain of the Canucks ahead of the CONCACAF Gold Cup the following year!

DEFOE

Even though he's had an amazing career, the 2020-21 Scottish Prem was only the second trophy the striker has won in his career. The other was the League Cup with Tottenham in 2007-08!

KENT

The rapid winger was named Barnsley's 2016-17 Young Player of the Season after impressing on loan from Liverpool in the Championship!

HELANDER

The giant Sweden centre-back used to play alongside Brentford's Pontus Jansson at Malmo!

KATIC

At 6ft 4in, the rock-solid centre-back is the tallest player at Rangers!

> Pick your five favourite Gers stars, send them to MATCH and you could win a mega prize!

COMPETITION

WIN! A FREE ONE-YEAR MATCH SUBSCRIPTION

PICK YOUR TOP 5 GERS HEROES!

For the chance to win this mind-blowing magazine subscription, just write down your five favourite Rangers players, fill out your contact details and email a photograph of this page to **match.magazine@kelsey.co.uk.** Closing date: January 31, 2022. What are you waiting for?

1.

2.

3.

4.

5.

NAME:

DATE OF BIRTH:

ADDRESS:

MOBILE:

EMAIL:

31

LUNDSTRAM

FACTPACK

Name: *John Lundstram*

D.O.B: *18 February, 1994*

Position: *Midfielder*

Country: *England*

Strongest Foot: *Right*

Top Skill: *Epic energy!*

Boot Brand: *Nike*

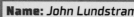

33

MIND-BLOWING You Tube CLIPS!

We check out some of the coolest videos on *RANGERS'* official YouTube channel! Get a load of these class clips...

RANGERS QR CODES EXPLAINED

This is a QR code - just scan it with your phone or tablet to watch each video clip on YouTube. Here's how to do it:

 Download and install a free QR Code reader from the app or android store.

 Hold your phone or tablet over the QR code and you'll be sent to the clip. Easy!

▶ GOAL ★ Alfredo Morelos ★ Rangers 1-0 Legia Warsaw

It's one of the most watched goals on the club's channel, and it's easy to see why! Alfredo Morelos buried a header into the bottom corner of the net in injury time to send Rangers into the group stage of the Europa League in 2019! The atmosphere inside Ibrox that night was absolutely buzzing. Unbelievable!

▶ Behind The Scenes ★ Steven Gerrard ★ Rangers Manager

It's fair to say that a few eyebrows were raised over three years ago when Steven Gerrard was appointed by Rangers, but he's proved all of his doubters wrong! This awesome video goes straight to the heart of the action as The Gers appointed the ex-Liverpool and England hero as their new gaffer. Quality!

▶ FEATURE: Jimmy Bullard
★ You Know The Drill

If you watch Soccer AM on Sky Sports regularly, then you'll know exactly what this wicked video is all about! Jimmy Bullard visits a different club every week and goes head-to-head with a few first-team players in a variety of epic training drills. This video looks behind the scenes from when he visited Auchenhowie back in 2015!

▶ We Are Rangers
★ We Are Champions

If you're looking for something to really remember last season by, then this is the perfect video for you! Rangers have put together an amazing montage documenting last season's record-breaking 'Invincibles' campaign in the Scottish Premiership! Make sure you've got the tissues at the ready, it's going to be an emotional one!

▶ Ally McCoist
★ Ice Bucket Challenge

It feels like an age since the Ice Bucket Challenge was trending all over social media, so perhaps it's about time it came back? Anyway, this hilarious video shows former Rangers player and manager Ally McCoist giving it a go. Rather you than us, Ally!

▶ HIGHLIGHTS ★ Rangers Legends v Liverpool Legends

Have you ever known a player to play for both teams during a match? Well, that's exactly what Steven Gerrard did when a Rangers Legends XI took on a Liverpool Legends XI back in 2019! Gerrard turned out for both teams and was even jokingly booed by the home crowd as he represented Liverpool in the first half. LOL!

▶ RANGERS TROPHY DAY
★ Trophy Presentation

It was a long wait for Rangers to reclaim the Scottish Premiership title, so why not relive last season's trophy presentation all over again? Rangers have uploaded the full presentation to their YouTube channel – the whole video is just under an hour long – so you can sit back and enjoy it whenever you like. What an amazing day!

RANGERS BRAIN BUSTER!

How much do you know about The Gers?

1. Which English League One club did Rangers sign James Tavernier from in 2015?

2. True or False? Manager Steven Gerrard made over 150 appearances for England!

3. Who did Rangers beat 2–1 in their qualifying play-off for the 2020–21 Europa League?

4. What was the main colour of the club's away kit in 2020–21 – white, yellow or black?

5. How many times did Rangers beat rivals Celtic in 2020–21 – three, four or five times?

6. What year did goal machine Kemar Roofe join Rangers – 2018, 2019 or 2020?

7. Which country does midfield baller Glen Kamara play for?

8. Who was gaffer of Rangers before Steven Gerrard?

9. True or False? Rangers' epic Ibrox stadium is the largest football ground in Scotland!

10. Which of these isn't one of their nicknames – The Light Blues, The Teddy Bears or The Warriors?

1 ....
2 ....
3 ....
4 ....
5 ....
6 ....
7 ....
8 ....
9 ....
10 ....

WORDFIT

Fit 25 of the club's top appearance makers into this huge grid!

Archibald

Cairns

Cooper

Ferguson

Gough

Gray

Greig

Henderson

Jackson

Jardine

Johnstone

MacDonald

Manderson

McCloy

McCoist

McColl

McGregor

McKinnon

McLean

McPhail

McPherson

Meiklejohn

Morton

Smith

Young

ANSWERS ON PAGE 60

OLD FIRM HISTORY

We take a closer look at the Rangers v Celtic rivalry over the years!

OLD FIRM THROUGH THE YEARS!

BIGGEST DEFEAT!

Look away now, Gers fans, because the biggest-ever Old Firm margin of defeat came in 1957! The score was 2-0 going into the break, but a crazy second half of goals for Celtic saw them win 7-1 and seal the League Cup trophy!

FIRST OLD FIRM!

The clubs met for the first time way back in 1888 during a friendly match that Celtic won 5-2, although it isn't recognised as an official game! A commentator said the teams were like "two old, firm friends", which is where some people think the name 'Old Firm' actually comes from!

1888

1909

1957

1989

CUP CRAZY!

The 1909 Scottish Cup Final ended 2-2! There were no penalties or extra-time in those days, so the game had to be replayed a week later. However, after the replay ended 1-1, both sets of fans decided to invade the pitch, with the SFA deciding not to award the trophy to any team that year. It became known as the "Cup That No One Won"!

MO'S MOVE!

Mo Johnston scored 52 goals in 99 league games for Celtic before spending two years in France with Nantes! He decided to return to Glasgow, but this time to the men in blue, becoming just the second player to cross the Old Firm divide since World War II. It didn't go down well with either sides' sets of supporters!

MAD MAYHEM!

Old Firms are always one of the fiercest fixtures on the footy calendar, but the 2011 Scottish Cup fifth round replay was one of the most ill-tempered in history! There were ten yellow cards and three red cards, with Ally McCoist and Neil Lennon scrapping on the sidelines as well!

RENEWED RIVALRY!

After rebuilding and regaining promotion back to the Scottish Premiership, Rangers were ready to renew their rivalry with Celtic ahead of the 2016-17 season! Their first league meeting for over four years didn't go to plan for The Gers, though – they lost 5-1 at Celtic Park, with Philippe Senderos being sent off on his debut for the club!

GERS' GLORY!

The 1998-99 title went down to the wire with Rangers needing to beat Celtic to lift the trophy! It ended up being total chaos, with fan invasions, sendings off and the referee being hit by something thrown from the crowd. The Gers still went on to win 3-0 and lift the league title!

2011

2016

1999

2021

2002

INVINCIBLES!

Celtic started the 2020-21 season with hopes of becoming the first Scottish side to win ten league titles in a row! Steven Gerrard's side were having none of it, though – they went the whole season unbeaten, matching The Bhoys' unbeaten campaign in 2016-17 and extending their top-flight titles tally to 55 – four more than Celtic. Get in!

CUP CLASSIC!

One of the great Old Firm Scottish Cup Finals ended in a thrilling 3-2 victory for Rangers thanks to a last-minute strike by Peter Lovenkrands! It was the Danish forward's second goal of the game, and came in the very final moments of the game as it was edging towards extra-time!

END OF THE OLD FIRM?

Rangers were in really bad financial trouble at the start of the 2010s and were eventually made to drop out of the league. They had to re-form in the Scottish fourth tier, but some Celtic fans said that it was the end of the traditional Old Firm derby and nowadays refer to the rivalry as the Glasgow Derby instead!

RANGERS LEGENDS!

We've taken a look back through the club's illustrious history to pick out nine of The Gers' best-ever players!

ALLY McCOIST

Even though his four-year spell as manager at Ibrox didn't end how he would've wanted, Ally McCoist remains a legendary figure at the club. The former striker comfortably remains Rangers' record goalscorer and won a mind-blowing nine consecutive league championships during his time at the club! He's been involved in a lot of media coverage over the last few years and has even previously appeared as a commentator on FIFA!

JOHN GREIG

Defensive legend Greig was voted as 'The Greatest Ever Ranger' by the club's supporters back in 1999, and it's easy to see why! There aren't many players that stick with one club nowadays, but Greig spent his entire career at Ibrox – as a player, manager and director! For that reason, it's no surprise that he's the club's record appearance maker in all competitions. He represented The Gers a whopping 755 times between 1961 and 1978. Wowzers!

RICHARD GOUGH

Kieran Tierney's £25 million move from rivals Celtic to Arsenal in 2019 makes him the most expensive Scotsman of all time, but Gough remains in the history books as the first Scot to be sold for over £1 million when he signed for Rangers back in 1987! The solid centre-back justified his transfer fee by captaining The Gers to their famous nine consecutive league championships and made over 300 league appearances during his two spells!

DAVIE COOPER

If the Netherlands' 1988 European Championship winning captain Ruud Gullit says you're the best player he ever played against, then you must be good! That's exactly what the Dutch football legend had to say about Cooper! He signed for Rangers in 1977 for £100,000 and went on to make 540 appearances over a 12-year spell with The Gers. He helped Rangers win countless trophies, including the Scottish Prem on three occasions!

BRIAN LAUDRUP

Regarded as one of the most talented players of his generation, Laudrup was undoubtedly one of the most well-known foreign players to ever play for Rangers! He played a key role as The Gers dominated in Scotland in the 1990s, and his epic performance in the final of the Scottish Cup in 1996 will live long in the memory for many of the club's supporters. He also played for Bayern Munich, AC Milan, Fiorentina, Chelsea and Ajax!

KRIS BOYD

When it comes to more recent times, there aren't many more legendary figures than prolific striker Kris Boyd! He joined Rangers in 2006 and was the club's top goalscorer in each of his five seasons at Ibrox. He remains the top goalscorer in the history of the Scottish Prem, with 167 goals in total! After spells in England, Turkey and the United States, Boyd return to Scotland to end his career with spells at Kilmarnock and back at Rangers!

BARRY FERGUSON

He's now plying his trade as a manager with Alloa Athletic in Scottish League One, but it wouldn't be a surprise to see Ferguson return to Ibrox in some capacity in the future – he's regarded as a proper legend for the two spells he enjoyed at Rangers! As well as helping The Gers reach the final of the UEFA Cup in 2008, he played an instrumental role in the treble-winning side of 2003 which saw him pick up the Scottish Football Writers' Association Footballer of the Year award! He's one of only four Rangers players to win the gong since the turn of the millennium – and the only one to win it twice!

ALLAN McGREGOR

If you're unfamiliar with some of the legendary figures on these two pages, then here's one you'll definitely recognise! Goalkeeper McGregor made his debut for The Gers back in 2002 and went on to make over 200 appearances during his first spell at Ibrox! After stints at Besiktas, Hull and Cardiff, McGregor returned to Ibrox in 2018 and remains a key figure in Steven Gerrard's record-breaking team – even though he'll turn 40 in 2022!

JIM BAXTER

If you go back in time to the 1960s, then there weren't many better players around than Baxter! He's regarded as one of Scotland's greatest-ever players, and Rangers were lucky enough to have him on their books for five years before returning for another brief spell before retiring. Baxter won ten trophies during his first spell at Ibrox and is undoubtedly one of the club's biggest legends!

BECOME A LEGEND!

Go all the way from Rangers' academy to a club legend! Use some coins as counters, grab a dice and battle your friends and family in this epic footy board game!

START ▶
KICK-OFF!
The player who rolls the highest number goes first!

2 ▶

3 ▶
LEGEND!
You've been scouted for Rangers' epic academy! Move forward three spaces!

4 ▶

5 ▶
FAIL!
Your youth team coach says your diet needs to improve! Move back a space!

6 ▶

◀ 12
FAIL!
A terrible Twitter gaffe gets you some negative headlines! Move back a space!

◀ 11

◀ 10
FAIL!
You get nutmegged by Joe Aribo in training! Move back four spaces!

◀ 9

◀ 8
LEGEND!
You earn your first professional contract at Ibrox! Move forward three spaces!

◀ 7

13 ▶

14 ▶
LEGEND!
MATCH magazine profiles you as a "Wonderkid To Watch"! Move forward two spaces!

15 ▶
FAIL!
You miss out on your debut due to a niggling knee injury! Move back two spaces!

16 ▶

17 ▶

18 ▶
LEGEND!
You're brought on as a sub for John Lundstram for your debut! Move forward four spaces!

◀ 24
LEGEND!
The fans invent a catchy new chant for you! Move forward two spaces!

◀ 23

◀ 22

◀ 21
LEGEND!
You score your first-ever goal for the club! Move forward two spaces!

◀ 20
FAIL!
Rangers legend Ally McCoist criticises your potential! Move back one space!

◀ 19

25 ▶
FAIL!
You react badly to getting subbed and lose the fans' respect! Move back three spaces!

26 ▶

27 ▶
LEGEND!
You win the Young Player of the Year award! Move forward four spaces!

28 ▶

29 ▶
FAIL!
The manager tells you you're not training hard enough! Move back six spaces!

30 ▶
LEGEND!
You're given your favourite shirt number! Move forward one space!

◀ 36

◀ 35
LEGEND!
You score in the Champions League group stage! Move forward three spaces!

◀ 34
FAIL!
You get a record low score on a Gers quiz on their YouTube channel! Move back three spaces!

◀ 33

◀ 32
FAIL!
You lose your cool during an interview when your form is questioned! Move back four spaces!

◀ 31

37 ▶
LEGEND!
You score a perfect hat-trick against Celtic! Move forward three spaces!

38 ▶

39 ▶
FAIL!
You try a Panenka penalty in the Old Firm derby but the keeper saves it! Move back three spaces!

40 ▶

41 ▶
FAIL!
An old photo emerges of you as a child in full Celtic kit! Move back five spaces!

WINNER!
YOU'RE A RANGERS LEGEND – YOU'LL GET A STATUE!

DAVIS

FACTPACK

Name: Steven Davis
D.O.B: 1 January, 1985
Position: Midfielder
Country: Northern Ireland
Strongest Foot: Right
Top Skill: Pinpoint passing!
Boot Brand: Nike

43

Allan McGregor **Ryan Jack** **Ianis Hagi** **Nathan Patterson**

ODD ONE OUT!

Which one of these Rangers heroes wasn't born in Scotland?

Scott Wright **Jake Hastie**

5 QUESTIONS ON...
IBROX

1 On which side of the River Clyde can you find the ace ground – North or South?

2 What is Ibrox Stadium's full capacity – over 50,000 or under 50,000?

3 True or False? Ibrox has also been used as a concert venue!

4 When was Ibrox first opened – 1889, 1899, 1909, 1919 or 1929?

5 True or False? The stadium's record attendance of 118,567 was set back in 1939!

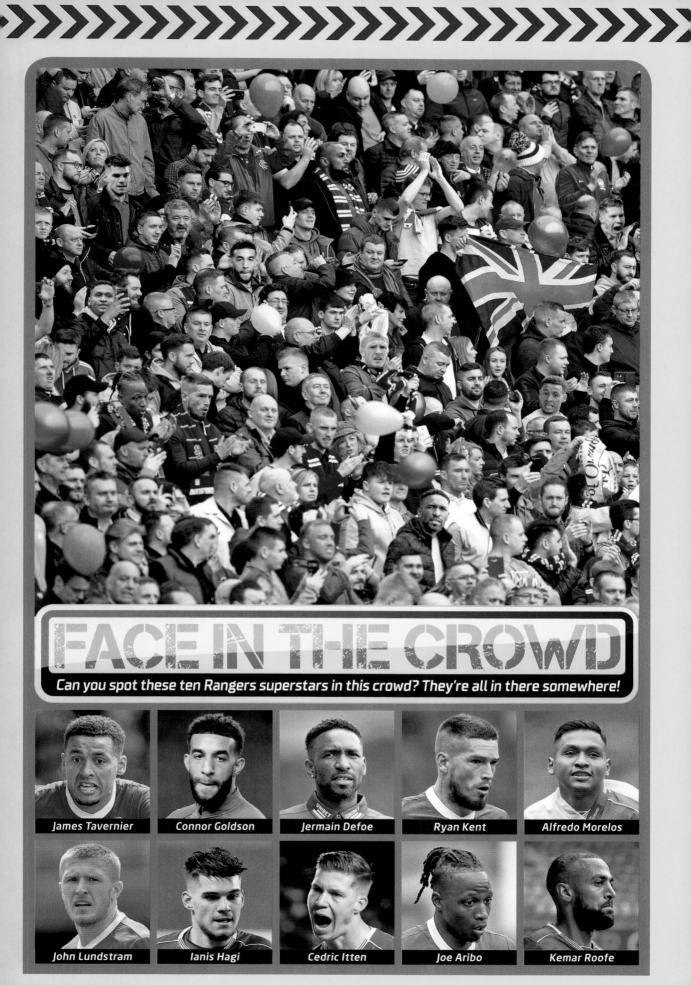

FACE IN THE CROWD

Can you spot these ten Rangers superstars in this crowd? They're all in there somewhere!

James Tavernier

Connor Goldson

Jermain Defoe

Ryan Kent

Alfredo Morelos

John Lundstram

Ianis Hagi

Cedric Itten

Joe Aribo

Kemar Roofe

ANSWERS ON PAGE 60

STAT ATTACK!

Get a load of RANGERS' all-time league appearance makers, goal records, social media followers and loads more!

7

Nobody was named Scottish Prem Man of the Match more times than Rangers' James Tavernier in 2020–21!

92

No team scored more league goals in 2020–21 than Rangers' 92 – and they were also the league's second-most accurate passers!

HOW THEY SCORED IN THE SCOTTISH PREM IN 2020–21

OPEN PLAY	SET-PIECES	OWN GOALS
65	14	5

PENALTIES	COUNTER ATTACK
7	1

TOP LEAGUE APPEARANCE MAKERS

John Greig   Sandy Jardine

Sandy Archibald	513
John Greig	498
David Meiklejohn	490
Dougie Gray	490
Sandy Jardine	451

90.7%

Glen Kamara had an incredible 90.7% pass completion rate in the 2020–21 league season – higher than any other team-mate!

TOP EUROPA LEAGUE APPEARANCE MAKERS

ALLAN McGREGOR
61

CONNOR GOLDSON
45

ALFREDO MORELOS
45

JAMES TAVERNIER
43

SCOTT ARFIELD
41

90 RB
TAVERNIER
97 PAC	90 DRI
87 SHO	87 DEF
90 PAS	94 PHY

20K+

That's how many coins you'll need to pick up James Tavernier's Team of the Season FIFA 21 card!

41

Rangers' defeat to Dundee United in August was their first loss in 41 Scottish Prem matches!

23

Nobody has scored more goals for Rangers in the Europa League than Alfredo Morelos!

Instagram

🔍 Search

stevengerrard ✔ [Follow] [⌄] •••

1,138 posts   9.2m followers   544 following

Steven Gerrard
Official Instagram Account of Steven Gerrard.

9M

Rangers gaffer Steven Gerrard has well over 9 million followers on Instagram!

facebook
793k
LIKES

rangersfc

525k
FOLLOWERS

RANGERS' NEXT GENERATION!

We take a closer look at five of the hottest young footy talents who are ready to become the future of the reigning Scottish champions!

CALVIN BASSEY

LEFT-BACK

The all-action, powerhouse left-back – who joined Rangers from Leicester's academy in 2020 – is mega versatile, having also filled in at centre-back in the past! The Italian-born ace, who is eligible to play for Italy, England and Nigeria, has a massive engine on him and will provide huge competition for Borna Barisic in 2022!

KIERAN WRIGHT

GOALKEEPER

The young keeper looks like a future Rangers No.1 in the making! Just like the player he's eventually looking to replace, Allan McGregor, he's had a couple of spells out on loan to further his footy education – including at Partick Thistle in 2020-21 where he won the club's Player of the Month award in November 2020!

NATHAN PATTERSON

RIGHT-BACK

The sky's the limit for Patterson, who was a shock call-up to Scotland's Euro 2020 squad last summer! Rangers boss Steven Gerrard is so impressed by his quality and potential that he's tried experimenting with his formation and system to try to fit both Patterson and club captain James Tavernier into the same team!

STEPHEN KELLY

MIDFIELDER

The 21-year-old has already been hailed as 'the future of Rangers' after some mega impressive displays during pre-season in the summer of 2021! He already plays with the maturity of a seasoned pro, and he's got the perfect role model to learn from with Steven Gerrard being a world-class midfielder during his playing days!

SCOTT WRIGHT

WINGER

Wright joined from Aberdeen in February 2021 when Steven Gerrard called him a 'project' signing. So far he's making top progress – he made his mark at the start of this season by scoring in Rangers' opening Prem game versus Livingston, and also started both ties against Malmo in the Champions League qualifiers!

ACADEMY SUPERSTARS!

Check out five of the best graduates to make it out of The Gers' academy in recent years!

Alan Hutton

The right-back played over 100 times for Rangers and is their record sale – joining Tottenham for £9m back in 2008!

Allan McGregor

The current No.1 is a proper club legend! After leaving Ibrox in 2012 with close to 300 appearances, he returned in 2018!

Billy Gilmour

The pass master is the future of Scotland's midfield! Gers fans are still gutted Chelsea poached him from their academy!

Barry Ferguson

The former Scottish Footballer of the Year spent the majority of his career at Rangers, captaining both his club and country!

Steven Naismith

The 51-times capped Scotland forward left Rangers' academy for Kilmarnock in 2002, before returning to Ibrox five years later!

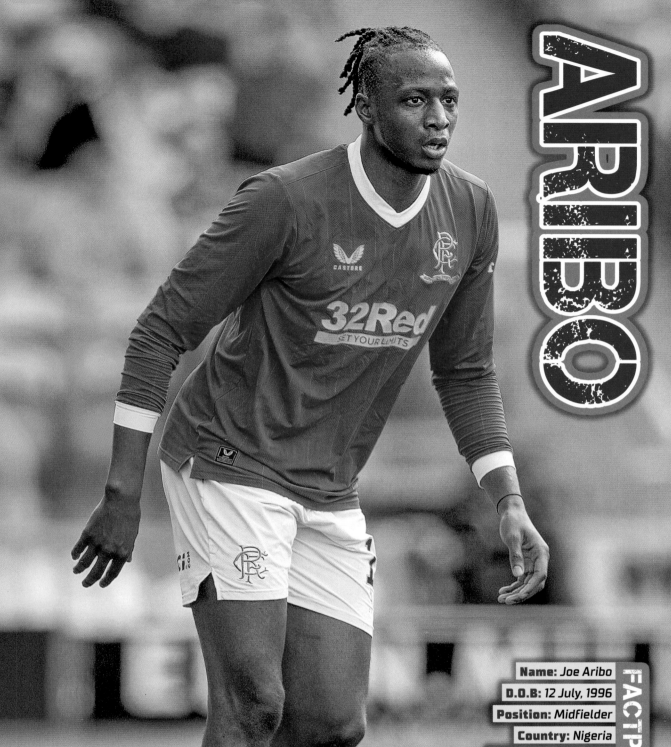

ARIBO

BIG '10

Test your knowledge of the Scottish champions! Can you get all ten right?

1 How old is awesome hitman Kemar Roofe – under 30 or over 30?

2 How many times has Allan McGregor won the Scottish Prem?

3 True or False? Rangers are the oldest football club in Scotland!

4 How many times did gaffer Steven Gerrard win the Champions League?

5 How many times did Rangers win the European Cup Winners' Cup?

6 How many goals did Ryan Kent score in the 2020–21 Europa League – two, three, four or five?

7 Who did Rangers concede their first Scottish Prem goal against in 2020–21?

8 What boot brand does Alfredo Morelos wear?

9 What is the base colour of Rangers' socks in 2021–22?

10 How many times have The Gers won the Scottish title?

1 point for each correct answer!

MY SCORE /10

1. Filip Helander

2. Connor Goldson

3. Steven Davis

NAME THE CLUB

Can you name the clubs Rangers signed these top-class footballers from?

4. Glen Kamara

5. Kemar Roofe

6. Scott Arfield

SPOT THE BALL!

Mark where you think the ball should be in this epic action pic!

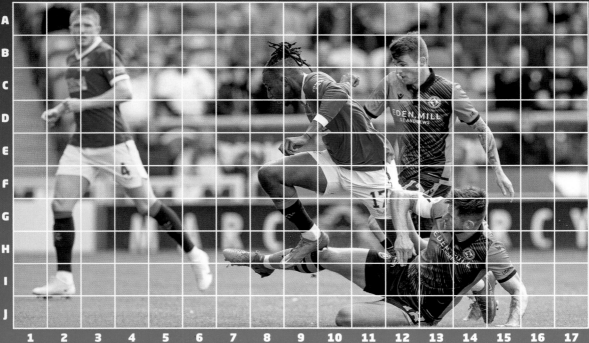

2021-22 FIRST TEAM SQUAD

GOALKEEPERS

No.	Player	League Games/Goals 2020-21	Signed from
1	Allan McGregor	27/0	Hull, 2018
13	Andy Firth	0/0	Barrow, 2019
28	Robby McCrorie	N/A	Academy
33	Jon McLaughlin	11/0	Sunderland, 2020
54	Kieran Wright	N/A	Academy

James Tavernier

DEFENDERS

No.	Player	League Games/Goals 2020-21	Signed from
2	James Tavernier	33/12	Wigan, 2015
3	Calvin Bassey	8/0	Leicester, 2020
5	Filip Helander	22/1	Bologna, 2019
6	Connor Goldson	38/4	Brighton, 2018
15	Jack Simpson	5/0	Bournemouth, 2021
16	Nathan Patterson	7/0	Academy
19	Nikola Katic	0/0	Slaven Belupo, 2018
26	Leon Balogun	19/0	Wigan, 2020
31	Borna Barisic	33/1	Osijek, 2018

MIDFIELDERS

No.	Player	League Games/Goals 2020-21	Signed from
4	John Lundstram	N/A	Sheff. United, 2021
7	Ianis Hagi	33/7	Genk, 2020
8	Ryan Jack	19/2	Aberdeen, 2017
10	Steven Davis	35/0	Southampton, 2019
14	Ryan Kent	37/10	Liverpool, 2019
17	Joe Aribo	31/7	Charlton, 2019
18	Glen Kamara	33/1	Dundee, 2019
21	Brandon Barker	10/2	Man. City, 2019
22	Juninho Bacuna	N/A	Huddersfield, 2021
24	Nnamdi Ofoborh	N/A	Bournemouth, 2021
27	Stephen Kelly	N/A	Academy
37	Scott Arfield	28/4	Burnley, 2018

Ryan Kent

FORWARDS

No.	Player	League Games/Goals 2020-21	Signed from
9	Jermain Defoe	15/4	Bournemouth, 2020
11	Cedric Itten	27/4	St. Gallen, 2020
20	Alfredo Morelos	29/12	HJK Helsinki, 2017
23	Scott Wright	9/1	Aberdeen, 2021
25	Kemar Roofe	24/14	Anderlecht, 2020
30	Fashion Sakala	N/A	Oostende, 2021

Squad correct up to August 25, 2021.

2021-22 HOME SHIRT

Take a closer look at Rangers' 2021-22 home threads...

This season's home shirt is a very special one as it features its iconic scroll crest in gold to commemorate the club's 150th anniversary!

Its classic V-neck design is inspired by some of the club's most popular and iconic kits from the '50s and '60s worn by the likes of Jim Baxter!

The club's shorts are white and goes well with this year's black socks which have a red strip at the top!

On top of all that, the shirt includes state-of-the-art lightweight, high stretch and breathable fabric, to maximise performance and comfort!

DESIGN YOUR

Create your own epic kits using the blank templates below!

THIRD KIT

GOALKEEPER KIT

LOVE MATCH?
GET IT DELIVERED EVERY FORTNIGHT!

6 ISSUES FOR JUST £6!*

PACKED EVERY ISSUE WITH...

- ★ Red-hot gear
- ★ News & gossip
- ★ Stats & quizzes
- ★ Massive stars
- ★ Posters & pics
- & loads more!

HOW TO SUBSCRIBE TO MATCH!

CALL 📱
01959 543 747
QUOTE: MATRA22

ONLINE 🖱
SHOP.KELSEY.CO.UK/ MATRA22

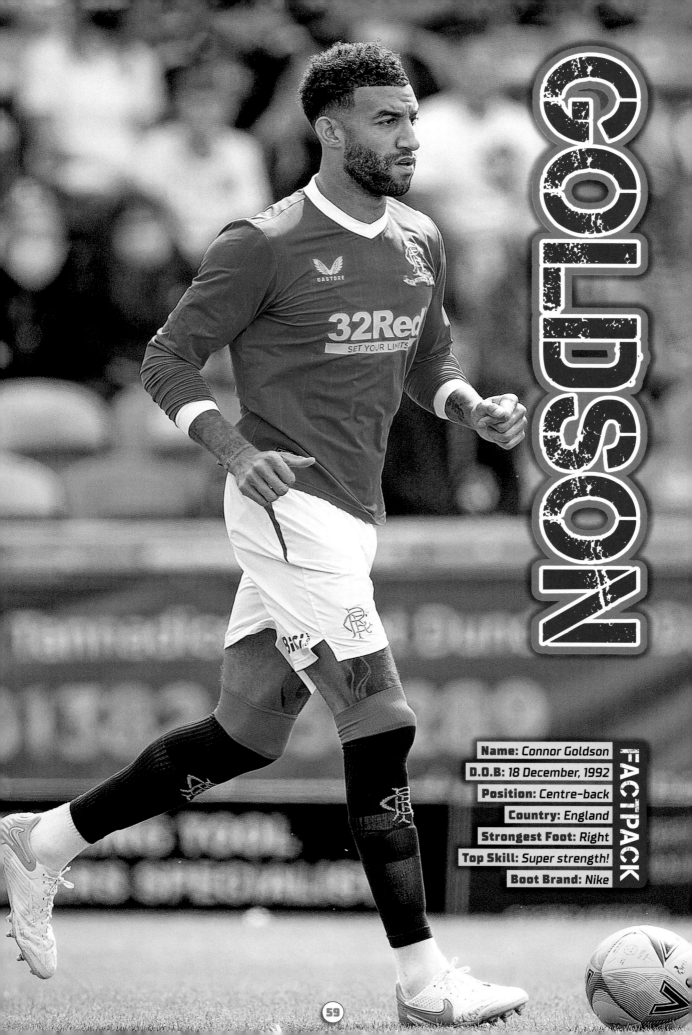

GOLDSON

FACTPACK

Name: Connor Goldson
D.O.B: 18 December, 1992
Position: Centre-back
Country: England
Strongest Foot: Right
Top Skill: Super strength!
Boot Brand: Nike

Wordsearch P18

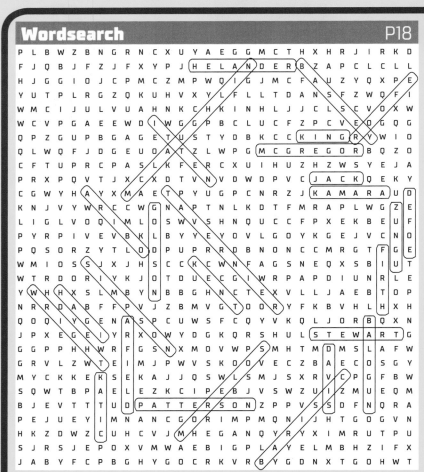

Action Replay P19

1. Scottish Premiership
2. Allan McGregor
3. False
4. Kemar Roofe
5. Rangers 2-1 Celtic
6. From open play
7. Callum McGregor
8. False
9. Rangers

Name The Team P27

1. Borna Barisic
2. Joe Aribo
3. Leon Balogun
4. Connor Goldson
5. Filip Helander
6. Allan McGregor
7. Ianis Hagi
8. Alfredo Morelos
9. Steven Davis
10. Glen Kamara
11. Ryan Kent

Spot The Difference P26

Rangers Brain-Buster P36

1. Wigan
2. False
3. Galatasaray
4. White
5. Four
6. 2020
7. Finland
8. Graeme Murty
9. False
10. The Warriors

Odd One Out P44

1. Ianis Hagi

Ibrox Quiz P44

1. South
2. Over 50,000
3. True
4. 1899
5. True

Wordfit P37

Face In The Crowd P45

Big 10 P52

1. Under 30
2. Four
3. False
4. Once
5. Once
6. Three
7. Hibernian
8. Nike
9. Black
10. 55

Name The Club P53

1. Bologna
2. Brighton
3. Southampton
4. Dundee
5. Anderlecht
6. Burnley

Spot The Ball P53

J3

ROLL OF HONOUR

EUROPEAN CUP WINNERS' CUP
1971-72

SCOTTISH PREMIERSHIP
1890-91, 1898-99, 1899-1900, 1900-01, 1901-02, 1910-11, 1911-12, 1912-13,
1917-18, 1919-20, 1920-21, 1922-23, 1923-24, 1924-25, 1926-27, 1927-28,
1928-29, 1929-30, 1930-31, 1932-33, 1933-34, 1934-35, 1936-37, 1938-39,
1946-47, 1948-49, 1949-50, 1952-53, 1955-56, 1956-57, 1958-59, 1960-61,
1962-63, 1963-64, 1974-75, 1975-76, 1977-78, 1986-87, 1988-89, 1989-90,
1990-91, 1991-92, 1992-93, 1993-94, 1994-95, 1995-96, 1996-97, 1998-99,
1999-2000, 2002-03, 2004-05, 2008-09, 2009-10, 2010-11, 2020-21

SCOTTISH CHAMPIONSHIP
2015-16

SCOTTISH LEAGUE ONE
2013-14

SCOTTISH LEAGUE TWO
2012-13

SCOTTISH CUP
1893-94, 1896-97, 1897-98, 1902-03, 1927-28, 1929-30, 1931-32, 1933-34,
1934-35, 1935-36, 1947-48, 1948-49, 1949-50, 1952-53, 1959-60, 1961-62,
1962-63, 1963-64, 1965-66, 1972-73, 1975-76, 1977-78, 1978-79, 1980-81,
1991-92, 1992-93, 1995-96, 1998-99, 1999-2000, 2001-02, 2002-03,
2007-08, 2008-09

SCOTTISH LEAGUE CUP
1946-47, 1948-49, 1960-61, 1961-62, 1963-64, 1964-65, 1970-71, 1975-76,
1977-78, 1978-79, 1981-82, 1983-84, 1984-85, 1986-87, 1987-88, 1988-89,
1990-91, 1992-93, 1993-94, 1996-97, 1998-99, 2001-02, 2002-03, 2004-05,
2007-08, 2009-10, 2010-11

SCOTTISH CHALLENGE CUP
2015-16

EMERGENCY WAR LEAGUE
1939-40

EMERGENCY WAR CUP
1939-40

SOUTHERN LEAGUE
1940-41, 1941-42, 1942-43, 1943-44, 1944-45, 1945-46

SOUTHERN LEAGUE CUP
1940-41, 1941-42, 1942-43, 1944-45

GLASGOW LEAGUE
1895-96, 1897-98

GLASGOW CUP
1893, 1894, 1897, 1898, 1900, 1901, 1902, 1911, 1912, 1913, 1914, 1918, 1919, 1922,
1923, 1924, 1925, 1930, 1932, 1933, 1934, 1936, 1937, 1938, 1940, 1942, 1943,
1944, 1945, 1948, 1950, 1954, 1957, 1958, 1960, 1969, 1971, 1975 (shared),
1976, 1979, 1983, 1985, 1986, 1987

VICTORY CUP
1946

SUMMER CUP
1942

GLASGOW MERCHANTS CHARITY CUP
1878-79, 1896-97, 1899-1900, 1903-04, 1905-06, 1906-07, 1908-09, 1910-11,
1918-19, 1921-22, 1922-23, 1924-25, 1927-28, 1928-29, 1929-30, 1930-31,
1931-32, 1932-33, 1933-34, 1938-39, 1939-40, 1940-41, 1941-42, 1943-44,
1944-45, 1945-46, 1946-47, 1947-48, 1950-51, 1954-55, 1956-57, 1959-60